The Way to School

Rosemary McCarney with Plan International

Second Story Press

You probably enjoy going to school.

Even if you have a bad day now and then, wouldn't you miss it if you could never go?

Did you know that lots and lots of kids around the world would love to go to school but can't?

Some are very poor and must work to help their families.

Philippines

Japan

Sometimes disasters such as earthquakes, tsunamis

and typhoons destroy schools.

But whenever possible, kids try to make their way to school.

Maybe like you, they walk, or ride, or take the bus.

But for many children, the way to school is not that easy.

It can be long and hard and even scary.

United States

Philippines

What if there was a river in your way? Would you bravely wade across…

Cambodia

paddle across…

Indonesia

float across…

Nepal

Nepal

Colombia

or fly across?

China

Sometimes the only way to school is around a mountain…

China

through a
long tunnel…

or over a high cliff!

China

China

China

China

In many places, animals take children to school.
A donkey is perfect if the way is high and rocky.

An ox can pull a cartful of friends.

A water buffalo will take its time.

A dog team is useful
when you are in a rush,
and there is no road!

When there is no drinking water at school, some children must carry their own. A basin of water is much heavier than books!

Ghana

Would you be willing to take your own desk to school?
If there was nothing to sit on, you might.

China

When rains come and waters rise, a temporary bridge can get you there.
This one is low and quite safe.

Indonesia

This bridge was high once, but now it has collapsed and is very dangerous. These children use it to and from school each day.

Philippines

Sometimes a single wire becomes a bridge…

and sometimes a few bamboo poles must do.

Whether your way to school
is long and lonely,

Tanzania

Haiti

short and friendly,

Philippines

wide and wet,

Laos

narrow and dry,

India

or rugged and cold and
slippery and high…

Haiti

…what matters is that you get there.
It's always worth the journey!

Library and Archives Canada Cataloguing in Publication

McCarney, Rosemary A., author
The way to school / Rosemary McCarney with Plan
International.

ISBN 978-1-927583-78-4 (bound)

1. School children—Developing countries—Social conditions—
Juvenile literature. 2. School children—Transportation—Developing
countries—Juvenile literature. 3. School children—Developing
countries—Juvenile literature. 4. Students—Developing countries—Social
conditions—Juvenile literature. 5. Students—Transportation—Developing
countries—Juvenile literature. 6. Students—Developing countries—
Juvenile literature. I. Plan (Organization), author II. Title.

LC208.M33 2015   j372.9172'4   C2015-902638-5

Copyright © 2015 Rosemary McCarney
with Plan International Canada Inc.

*Second Story Press gratefully acknowledges the support of the
Ontario Arts Council and the Canada Council for the Arts for our
publishing program. We acknowledge the financial support of
the Government of Canada through the Canada Book Fund.*

Printed and bound in China

ONTARIO ARTS COUNCIL
CONSEIL DES ARTS DE L'ONTARIO
an Ontario government agency
un organisme du gouvernement de l'Ontario

Canada Council   Conseil des Arts
for the Arts   du Canada

Published by
Second Story Press
20 Maud Street, Suite 401
Toronto, Ontario, Canada
M5V 2M5
www.secondstorypress.ca

Acknowledgments

Many thanks for the photographers across Plan who provided these
beautiful images of the work we do and for the other photojournalists
whose pictures tell the story of determined kids wanting to get to
school no matter what. Special thanks to Jen Albaugh for helping
me locate photos that would tell the story well and ensuring that
we selected the best of the best that captured the determination
and energy of school kids everywhere. It takes many hands to
create a compelling book like *The Way to School* — the writer, the
photographers, and gifted editors and a passionate publisher like
Second Story Press. Together, magic for young readers is created.
—Rosemary McCarney

Photo Credits

Cover: (front) Saikat Mojumder/Plan
(back) Mark Foster, Asti Alanna De
Guzman, Mikko Toivonen/Plan
Page 3: Mardy Halcon/Plan
Page 4: Richard Jones/Sinopix
Page 5: Jane Rivera/Plan
Page 7: © iStock/Purdue9394
Page 8: Asti Alanna De Guzman
Page 9: Mark Foster
Page 10: Iggoy el Fitra
Page 11: (top left) David Sowerwine/
Village Tech Solutions, (top right)
Tyler Miller/Village Tech Solutions,
(bottom) Fanny Gauret/Learning World
Euronews
Page 12: HAP/Quirky China News/REX
Page 13: HAP/Quirky China News/REX
Page 14: (left) HAP/Quirky China News/
REX, (right) HAP/Quirky China News/
REX
Page 15: HAP/Quirky China News/REX
Page 16: MM/Color China Photo/Sipa
Page 17: Wen Leonardo/Sipa Press
Page 18: Andrey
Page 19: DEDDEDA
Page 20: Nyani Quarmyne/Plan

Page 21: Mikko Toivonen/Plan
Page 22: Quirky China News/REX
Page 23: Iggoy el Fitra
Page 24: Asti Alanna De Guzman
Page 25: Iggoy el Fitra
Page 26: James Stone/Plan
Page 27: Rose-Carmille Jeudy/Plan
Page 28: Asti Alanna De Guzman
Page 29: Jim Holmes/Plan
Page 30/31: Timothy Allen
Page 32: Ben Depp/Plan